VERONICA RED

— Sun Child —

COSMIC LIGHT

Copyright © 2020 by Veronica Red. 783911

All rights reserved. No part of this book may be
reproduced or transmitted in any form or by
any means, electronic or mechanical, including
photocopying, recording, or by any information
storage and retrieval system, without permission in
writing from the copyright owner.

To order additional copies of this book, contact:
    Xlibris
    1-800-455-039
    www.xlibris.com.au
    Orders@Xlibris.com.au

ISBN: Softcover   978-1-7960-0909-5
         EBook   978-1-7960-0908-8

Print information available on the last page

Rev. date: 02/24/2020

In loving memory of

Pamela Colman Smith and Helen Keller

Feeling my eyes beginning to open, I
quickly shut them tight.
Bursting sunbeams warming my face,
bathing in cosmic light,

The loud whistling birds outside informing
there is a window open,
Letting me know the animal kingdom
has also been awoken.

My eyes are still closed as I drift off into a
deep thought,
Wondering how the sun sees us here on
planet Earth.

The solar waves warming us with their
magnificent heat and light,
Spreading themselves over the entire
planet, greeting every day with new life.

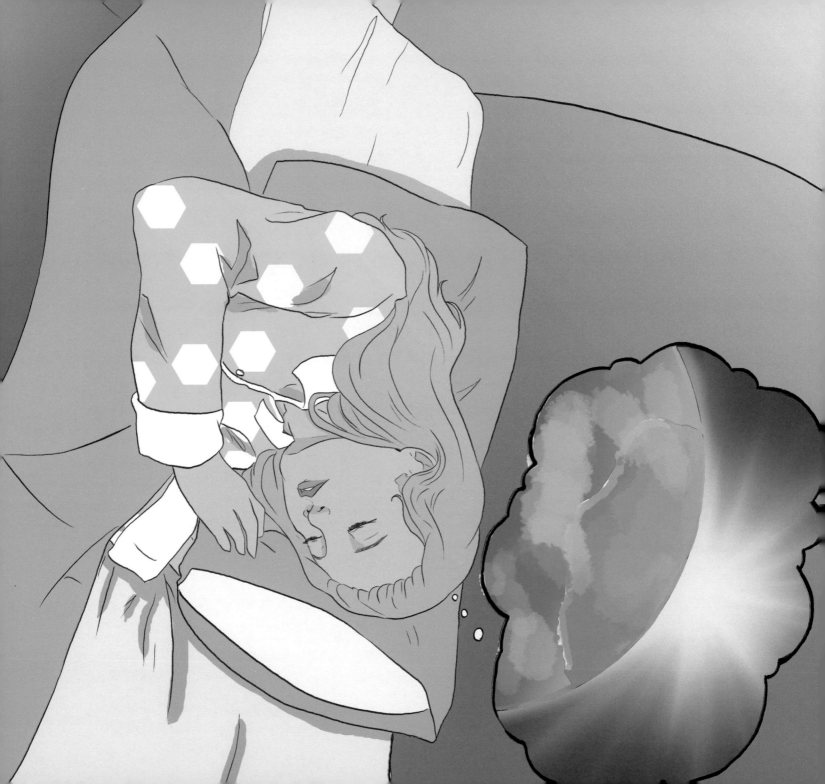

The special bond between the moon and sun is such a phenomenal union, With night and day shared equally while our planet enjoys a holy communion.

Moon and sun are balanced at just the right distance, appearing the same size, Neither coming or going within our atmosphere—a clever disguise.

Up in space is this powerful sun as our Earth revolves around it, illuminating everything it touches so that we may prosper and benefit.

Whether high in the sky or low on the horizon, it shares its stunning light. Split apart the shards of colour as we glimpse this dazzling delight.

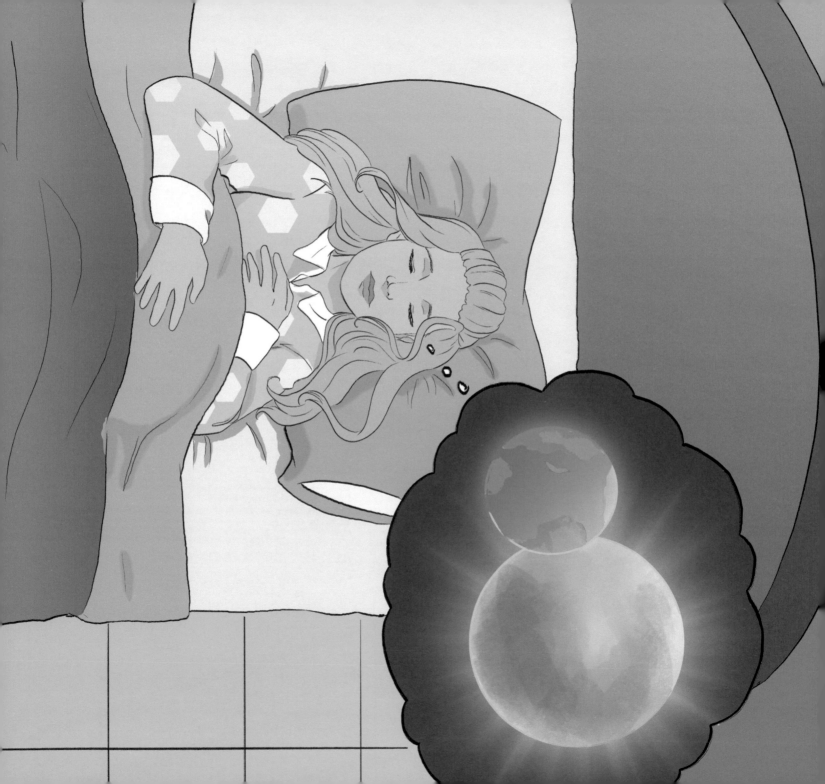

An intelligent solar energy that is not created by any human,
It never sleeps, eats, or requires anything from us, this magical bright beacon.

Just a perfectly balanced store of frequencies generated and shared worldwide,
We have found a way to foresee its arrival with predicted movement clockwise.

Without the sun's rays there would be no
growth, no warmth or colour,
No energy for our growing green plants
that provide food and oxygen like no other.

Though there are billions of stars in space
just like our own sun,
This particular one at the centre of our
solar system is our number one.

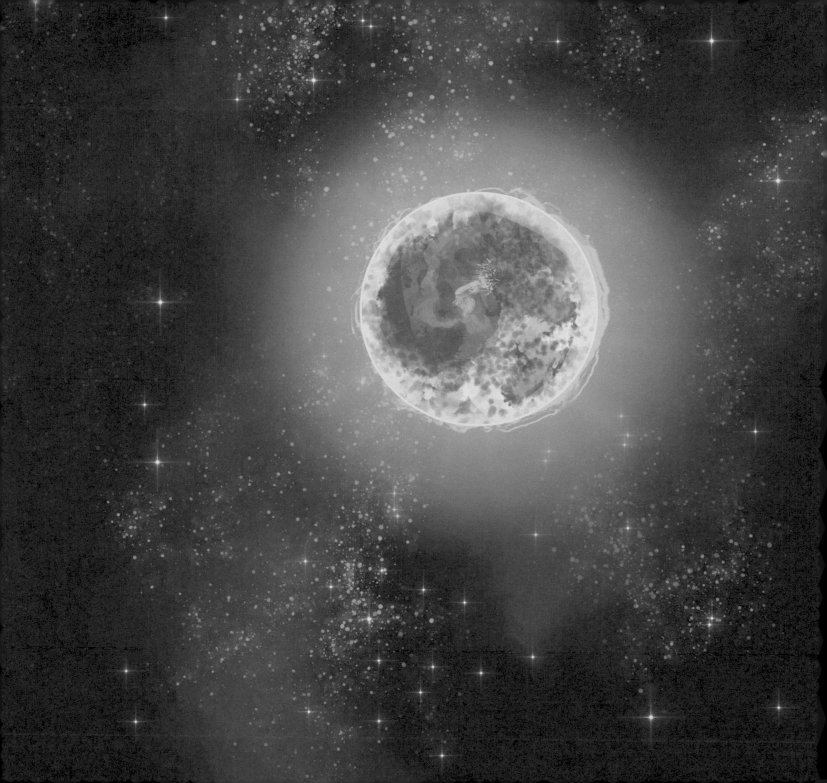

To give you an idea of just how large this
loving star is,
It is so large that about one million planet
Earths can fit comfortably in.

This enormous being reminds me of its
fierce and pure strength,
Stretching out to do its great work at such
intense wavelength.

I learned that one of the days in our week
is named after our sun.
Sunday is the day that reminds us of it
and also to have fun.

Patiently awaiting its arrival on the seventh
day of every week,
Celebrating the sun is a decision I made
that is somewhat unique.

Working on creating something new when the light hits the ground,
A vision of plants climbing to the top wearing fruits as if they are crowned.

The cosmic dance between the sun and Earth driving seasons, oceans, and weather,
The effects touching everything—minerals, animals, and humans all together.

Every little bit of this golden light is absorbed and never wasted,
Beautiful scenes being illuminated as if they have been painted.

Sometimes we need to protect ourselves, as the powerful rays can burn,
Teaching us to balance this whilst we create shade in return.

It's time to open my eyes, get up, and
enjoy what I see,
Feeling refreshed, confident, and
seemingly carefree.

Knowing I am lovingly protected and
balanced with each glorious ray,
I feel much stronger, more alive and
energized each and every day.

Printed in the United States
By Bookmasters